New Century Citizen

New Century Citizen

WHAT IS THE HIGHEST PRIORITY *for* HUMAN BEINGS?

DISCARD

Mary Wallstrom, M.Ed.

AUBERGINE PUBLISHING
San Diego, California

Acknowledgments

I would like to express my sincere gratitude to my parents, Carl and Claire, for always being there. Dad, thank you for providing for our family and showing me how to appreciate history. Mom, your unconditional love has deeply touched my heart and helped me through the most difficult times of my life.

I'd also like to acknowledge Peri Poloni, graphic designer extraordinaire, for your innovative contribution to this book and Laurie Gibson, for the quality of your editing skills and your helpful suggestions.

I have had some exceptional teachers along the way. Thank you, Dr. Sue Zgliczynski, for being a helpful guide and advisor as I progressed through graduate school. Thank you, Dr. Ronn Johnson, for sharing the wealth of your counseling expertise. Thank you, Dr. Anita Rogers, for always encouraging me. And thank you, Greg Williams, for being a trusted friend and colleague on whom I can always depend.

Finally, I give my heartfelt appreciation to Frank Salamone. I miss you everyday, grandpa. Thank you for your love and showing me how to appreciate the simple things in life.

This book is dedicated to every person who has ever struggled with making an important choice in their life.

Introduction

Choices. We make choices every day. Some choices, like what we choose to eat for dinner or what route we choose to take to work, have short-term effects. And some choices, like if we choose to marry, what occupation we choose to pursue, or where we choose to live, have long-term effects. These are examples of our personal choices. But we make choices as groups, too. As families we make choices – where we choose to go for vacation, how we choose to care for our elderly parents, etc. As corporate members we make choices – hiring policy choices, stock option plan choices, etc. As citizens of our country we make choices – how we choose to structure our

Introduction

government, how we choose to employ our education system.

And finally, there's the big picture. Our global choices. How we, as human beings, collectively choose to treat our children. How we choose to treat each other. How we choose to treat our home, our earth.

Oftentimes, it's difficult for me to fathom how my choices have any global impact. But I've realized that our civilization could not have reached its current status without the collective choices we make as human beings. These choices have created the world we live in.

Today we're bombarded with so much information on a daily basis about international activities that it's easy to become overloaded with data. Therefore I decided to step back, look at the big picture, and get some statistics on the choices

Introduction

we human beings are making that have gotten us to our current status. And then by looking at these statistics, see if it can be determined to which kind of choice we give the most importance. In other words, what is the highest priority on which we human beings choose to focus? And by discovering our highest priority, would we choose to stay the course or shift our priority? These are questions I intend to investigate in the pages of this book.

I have divided our global choices into eight categories: education, relationships, health, the environment, personal safety, peace, service, and money. The facts should allow us to see our current highest priority.

Before looking at the choices we're making, I felt it would be helpful to remind myself of our history and recall what we human beings have done

Introduction

to get us where we are today. We have accomplished a great deal. Below I have noted important milestones in significant areas of our development.

About 100,000 years ago, we human beings (Homo sapiens) emerged from the predecessors of our genus – Homo erectus and Homo habilis. Approximately 10,000 years ago, these humans succeeded in colonizing the inhabitable world. Ten thousand-year-old skeletons display evidence of violent death at this dawn of human civilization. At first, hunting and gathering was the way of life. This was succeeded by farming, which supported more people in a particular area. Towns and villages grew, surrounded by walls. Land and resource conflicts arose and by the time the first city-states emerged, armies were being assembled.

Introduction

A class of men became soldiers whose sole job was warfare.

- Agricultural milestones include the domestication of sheep, cattle, and pigs between 8500 BC and 7000 BC; the first irrigation in the Tigris and Euphrates Valley around 6000 BC; the first use of the plough in southeast Europe in approximately 4500 BC; the Marcian Aqueduct bringing water to Rome in 144 BC; and Carolus Linnaeus of Sweden developing a plant classification system in 1737 AD.

- Milestones in textiles include spinning and weaving in the Near East around 7000 BC; linen made in England in 1253 AD; the development of the silk industry by Italians living in Lyons, France, in 1315; a cotton factory established in Manchester, England, in 1640; and the arrival of the Singer sewing machine in 1851.

Introduction

- Household items began with pottery in the Near East around 7000 BC and progressed to oil lamps introduced in Greece in 230 BC; the use of coil springs in clocks by Brunelleschi of Italy in 1410 AD; the first flushing toilet invented by Sir John Harington in 1589; and the invention of the electric washing machine in 1907.

- The transportation evolution began when the first ships appeared on the Mediterranean around 5000 BC followed by wheeled vehicles (oxcarts, etc.) in central Europe in approximately 3500 BC; an early Roman road called the "Via Appia," which began in 312 BC; the invention of the first true steam engine by James Watt in 1777 AD; the first practical gas-burning automobile manufactured by Karl Benz in 1885; and the Wright Bros. powered air flight in 1903.

Introduction

- Important developments in communication started with the beginning of writing, done in the cuneiform style utilizing wedge-shaped strokes primarily inscribed on clay, around 3300 BC in Mesopotamia; the replacement of clay tablets with parchment in Persia in 460 BC; the introduction of the printing press by Gutenberg in 1450 AD; the invention of the telephone by Alexander Graham Bell in 1876; and the development of the television by John Logie Baird in 1925.

- Weaponry evolved from crude implements to flint knives around 3000 BC; to iron weapons used in North Africa around 700 BC; the first use of the cannon in Germany in 1324 AD; the first machine gun patented by James Puckle in 1718; use of the atomic bomb in 1945; and development of the stealth bomber in the 1970s.

Introduction

- Milestones in manufacturing include the first use of iron in Europe around 800 BC; the use of coal for smelting iron by the Chinese in the 4th century AD; the invention of the sawmill in 1328; the mass production of steel using the Bessimer process in 1856; and the development of the steam turbine by Charles Parsons in 1884.

- Important events in trade include the first coins struck from electrum (a natural alloy of gold and silver) in 700 BC; the founding of the Medici Bank in 1387 AD; the Stock Exchange founded in London in 1698; the introduction of income tax to Britain by William Pitt in 1799; and the legalization of trade unions in Britain in 1825.

- Advances in medicine began with Hippocrates's revolutionary ideas (e.g. the use of case studies) around 430 BC; the first public hospital in Rome in 362 AD; the discovery of the

Introduction

smallpox vaccine by Edward Jenner in 1796; the discovery of penicillin by Alexander Fleming in 1928; and the first human heart transplant performed by Christiaan Barnard in 1967.

- Technological mileposts include the use of the waterwheel throughout the Roman world around 50 BC; the use of coal gas as a source of lighting in 1691 AD; the invention of the electric cell by Alessandro Volta in 1800; the invention of the light bulb by Joseph Swan in 1878; and the building of the nuclear reactor by Enrico Fermi in 1942.

- Advances in science and mathematics include the use of the abacus in China around 190 AD; the creation of the temperature scale by Gabriel Fahrenheit in 1714; the publication of Charles Darwin's *The Origin of Species,* in 1858; the

Introduction

splitting of the atom by Ernest Rutherford in 1919; and the discovery of the structure of DNA in 1953.

- And finally, exploration milestones include the arrival of Italian Marco Polo in Peking in 1275 AD; Columbus landing at San Salvador in 1492; the completion of world circumnavigation by the Portuguese in 1522; the first man (Yuri Gargarin) launched into space in 1961; and the landing of Apollo 11 on the moon in 1969.

We've come a long way from the hunter-gatherers of 10,000 years ago. Our population has increased from 1 billion in 1820 AD to over 6 billion in 2003. The average life expectancy, worldwide, is 62 years for men and 70 years for women. We're living longer lives. We have the capability to communicate instantaneously with anyone at any point on the planet. We have the ability to save many more lives through advances in

Introduction

medicine. We have so much at our disposal as human beings.

We've arrived at the dawn of a new century. The canvas for the next 100 years is empty, awaiting new inventions and milestones. We can declare our resolutions for the new century now. We can reveal what it will take to become a new century citizen.

Now it's time to look at the statistics – the hard facts – that will illustrate how we're living our lives today and what we have chosen as our highest priority. Will this be the highest priority for a new century citizen?

Is EDUCATION our Highest Priority?

The Statistics

In the United States, 29% of high school students go on to attain a bachelor's degree. (2001 findings)[1]

Reading performance of students in the United States:
Grade 4 – 31% of students read at or above a proficient level.
Grade 8 – 33% of students read at or above a proficient level.
Grade 12 – 40% of students read at or above a proficient level. (1998 findings)[1]

Writing performance of students in the United States:

Grade 4 – 22% of students write at or above a proficient level.

Grade 8 – 25% of students write at or above a proficient level.

Grade 12 – 21% of students write at or above a proficient level. (1998 findings)[1]

SAT scores for U.S. students:

1966-1967 – average verbal score: 543
average math score: 516

2000-2001 – average verbal score: 506
average math score: 514[2]

Average beginning salary for teachers in the United States: $29,284. (2000 findings)[2]

Education

In 1961, 8% of all teachers in the United States were first-year teachers.
In 1996, 2.1% of all teachers in the United States were first-year teachers.[2]

The average yearly tuition, plus room and board, for a 4-year private university in the United States: $23,000.
The average yearly tuition, plus room and board, for a 4-year public university in the United States: $9,200. (2001-2002 findings)[1]

Approximately 115 million children in developing countries have never set foot in a school. (1999 findings)[3]

There are an estimated 1.4 billion illiterate adults in the world. (2003 findings)[4]

From the above statistics, one can objectively conclude the following:

Using reading as the primary criteria, about 25% of the world's population is uneducated. In the United States, less than one-third of high school students go on to graduate from college. Less than half of all students read and write at a proficient level. Students' verbal SAT scores have declined by 37 points over a 34-year period while math scores have remained fairly constant. Fewer students aspire to be teachers with a 6% decline in first year teachers over the last 38 years. And the cost of higher education in the United States is high – an average $36,800 for a public school degree; an average $92,000 for a private school degree.

If one were to use a 100-point grading scale, the state of global education would receive a grade

Education

of C, with 75% of the population considered literate. But there's one important distinction that needs to be taken into account: literacy statistics are calculated with basic reading skills as the criteria for a person to be considered literate. Would an individual with basic reading skills be considered educated? Wouldn't it be more appropriate to consider an educated individual to be one that reads at a proficient level? Statistics for the United States illustrate that only 40% of high school seniors read at or above a proficient level. From that statistic one could conclude that the true state of global education is more likely below the 75th percentile (with fewer people reading at a proficient level), thus receiving an even lower grade.

    I remember the excitement I felt when my second grade teacher gave me a gold star for a paper I submitted. I think it consisted of 5 simple sentences. But that gold star made me want to learn more. With less than half of high school seniors reading at a proficient level, the excitement for learning seems to have gotten lost somewhere along the way. And it's disheartening to come to terms with the fact that millions of the world's children haven't even had the opportunity to share in the elation of drinking in knowledge.

We can pour money into the education system for newer books or better classroom conditions, but would this encourage students to learn more? I think a child could learn even if the only classroom he had available was under a tree or in a small, thatched hut, as long as he had a teacher who inspired him. I think creating incentives for individuals to aspire to be teachers as well as encouraging current teachers to step up their level of enthusiasm to better motivate their students could

Education

be a good first step in re-igniting a child's passion for learning.

But since a student needs inspiration to encourage them to learn, does it not logically follow that teachers need inspiration as well to help them continue with their work? Greg Williams, a colleague of mine who works as a School-to-Career Coordinator in a San Diego inner-city school, shared with me some important problems that teachers have to deal with on a daily basis. He indicated that teachers not only have to plan and deliver their curriculum, but also have to deal with students who are disruptive during class, students who may have issues outside of class, students who don't want to learn, as well as uncooperative parents. Add to that the changes that are mandated each year by the school district and federal and state governments. Mr. Williams says, "Many teachers become overwhelmed and feel the profession no longer offers them the rewards they once experienced or anticipated."

I think a task force whose sole purpose was to inspire teachers to be the best motivators they can be, as well as help them deal with the added burdens which exist in the current educational system, would even further the goal to encourage students to learn more. This could help teachers keep that spark alive which can remind them of why they became a teacher in the first place. And keep alive that goal of a gold star for today's students. A new century citizen will be a well-educated human being.

Education

[1] National Center for Education Statistics, *The Condition of Education*

[2] National Center for Education Statistics, *Digest of Education Statistics*

[3] UNESCO Institute for Statistics

[4] CIA, *The World Factbook*

Are RELATIONSHIPS our Highest Priority?

The Statistics

The divorce rate in the United States is 53%. (1998 findings)[1]

In the United States, between 1970 and 1998, the proportion of children living in single parent homes more than doubled – from 12% to 28%.[2]

An estimated 13.5 million parents in the United States have custody of 21.7 million children under the age of 21 whose other parent lives elsewhere. (2000 findings)[1]

In the United States, 5.6 million custodial parents have no child support agreement. (2000 findings)[1]

In the United States, 75.8% of preschool children receive childcare from a source other than a relative – 59.7% from center-based programs; 16.1% from non-relatives. (1999 findings)[3]

The average wage of a childcare worker in the United States is $16,980. (2001 findings)[4]

In the United States, 25% of 4th – 8th graders (9-14 year olds) care for themselves regularly before or after school. (2001 findings)[5]

Child protective service agencies in the United States received reports on more than 3 million

Relationships

maltreated children. Eighty (80)% of the perpetrators were parents of the victim. Fifty two (52)% of victimized children were 7 or younger. As a result of maltreatment, an estimated 1,077 children died. (1996 findings)[2]

Nearly 800,000 children are reported missing each year in the United States, (more than 2,000 per day). The largest percentage are runaways, followed by family abductions. Non-family abductions total approximately 58,000 per year. (1999 findings)[6]

A total of 1 in 5 children in the United States, from 10 to 17 years of age, receive unwanted sexual solicitation online. (2001 findings)[7]

In the high school class of 2000 in the United States, 80% of students reported using alcohol; 54% of students reported using illicit drugs.[3]

In the United States, 46% of 10th graders reported using illicit drugs in their lifetime; 27% of 8th graders reported using illicit drugs in their lifetime. (2001 findings)[8]

In the United States, 29.1% of students had their first alcoholic drink (other than a few sips) before age 13. (2001 findings)[9]

In the United States, 30% of seniors reported they had 5 or more drinks in a row during the previous 2 weeks; 25% of 10th graders reported having 5 or more drinks in a row during the previous 2 weeks; 13% of 8th graders reported having 5 or more drinks

Relationships

in a row during the previous 2 weeks. (2001 findings)[5]

In the United States, 7.4% of high school seniors reported using the drug ecstasy during the last year. (2002 findings)[8]

In the United States, 30% of high school seniors reported smoking 1 or more cigarettes during the past 30 days; 21% of 10th graders reported smoking 1 or more cigarettes during the past 30 days; 12% of 8th graders reported smoking 1 or more cigarettes during the past 30 days. (2001 findings)[8]

In the United States, 4 million of the new cases of STDs (sexually transmitted diseases) each year occur in teens. (2000 findings)[10]

From the above statistics, one can objectively conclude the following:

In the United States, more than half of marriages fail. Close to 1/3 of today's children live in single parent homes. A total of 41% of custodial parents have no agreement on child support. More than 3/4 of today's parents who have children under 5 years of age entrust the care of their preschool children to someone other than a relative. The average wage for a childcare worker is $8.16 per hour. A total of 1/4 of middle-schoolers are home alone before or after school. More than half of maltreated children are 7 or younger. A significant number of children run away from home each year. A total of 20% of 10 – 17 year olds are approached online with unwanted sexual solicitation. Close to half of high school students use illicit drugs. More than 3/4 of seniors drink alcohol. A quarter of high

Relationships

schoolers report having 5 or more drinks in a row. And more than 1/4 of students had their first drink before age 13. Almost 1/3 of high school seniors smoke. Teens are practicing unsafe sex (as seen by the numbers of new cases of STD's).

These statistics clearly indicate that parents in the United States are spending less time with their children; this is reflected by the number of preschoolers and middle-schoolers who have no parental supervision during the day. This begs the question, could this fact be related to the significant number of teens now using drugs and alcohol? And since parents are spending less time with their children, are they also spending less time with their spouses? Could this be a contributing factor to the high divorce rate?

I consider myself fortunate that my mother was at home while I was growing up in the 1960's and 70's. She was there when I got home from school. She was there during summer break. She was there to care for me when I was ill. But our society has evolved in the last 30 years. More and more moms are working either for financial necessity or for self-fulfillment and the sense of accomplishment. Stay-at-home moms still exist, but oftentimes have to make financial sacrifices to allow them the opportunity to be there all day for their children.

With the significant number of teens using drugs and alcohol, it's clear that parents need to have more of a presence in their children's lives. How can this be done considering the constraints of a working parent's schedule? I think a collaboration would have to take place between the business community, the school districts, and parents to create a schedule that affords parents more time with their children. For example, if school districts could schedule classes from 8:00 am to 4:00 pm, businesses could comply with business hours rescheduled from 8:30 am to 3:30 pm. Although this would cut back a work day to 7 hours and extend a school day to 8 hours, working parents would now be available to be with their children both before and after school. This would not only give parents more time to be with their children, but would give spouses more time to spend together as well. More parental supervision will obligate a child to be more accountable for his actions. Businesses may not like the loss of work hours, but aren't more cohesive families worth it? A new century citizen encourages a united family.

[1]U.S. Census Bureau

[2] Office of Juvenile Justice and Delinquency Prevention, *Statistical Briefing Book*

[3] National Center for Education Statistics

[4] Bureau of Labor Statistics, *National Occupational Employment and Wage Estimates*

[5] Federal Interagency Forum on Child and Family Statistics, *America's Children 2002*

[6] U.S. Department of Justice, *National Incidence Studies of Missing, Abducted, Runaway, and Throwaway Children 2002*

[7] U.S. Department of Justice, *Highlights of the Youth Internet Safety Survey*

[8] Institute for Social Research, University of Michigan, *Monitoring the Future Study*

[9] National Institute on Alcohol Abuse and Alcoholism

[10] U.S. Department of Health and Human Services, *Healthy People 2010*

Is HEALTH our Highest Priority?

The Statistics

More than 44 million people in the United States do not have health insurance, including 11 million children. (1997 findings)[1]

In the United States, 76% of medium and large-sized corporations provide medical care benefits as opposed to 92% in 1989. (1997 findings)[2]

In the United States, 27% of children aged 19-35 months do not receive all recommended vaccines. (1998 findings)[1]

An estimated 3.8 million children in the United States have unmet dental needs because the family cannot afford care. (2002 findings)[3]

In the United States, 32% of prescription drug expenditures are paid out of pocket. (2000 findings)[3]

In the United States, an estimated 64% of adults ages 20-74 are overweight (a Body Mass Index greater than or equal to 25) and 31% of adults ages 20-74 are obese (a Body Mass Index greater than or equal to 30). In addition, 15% of children ages 6-19 are overweight. (2000 findings)[3]

Every day, an estimated 3,000 young persons under the age of 18 start smoking in the United States. (2000 findings)[1]

Health

Tobacco causes approximately 13,500 deaths per day worldwide. (2003 findings)[4]

Globally, 47.5% of men smoke, 10.3% of women smoke. (2003 findings)[4]

In the United States, an estimated 9,806,000 males abuse or are dependent upon alcohol as defined by DSM-IV. Females who abuse or are dependent upon alcohol total 3,953,000. (1992 findings)[6]

In the year 2000, there were 13,050 alcohol-related traffic fatalities in the United States.[6]

Worldwide, alcohol causes 1.8 million deaths per year. (2002 findings)[5]

In the United States, half of all clients in substance abuse treatment centers receive treatment for both alcoholism and drug abuse. (2000 findings)[3]

Each day in the United States, 17 organ transplant candidates die because not enough organs are available. Waiting list candidates exceed 80,000. (2002 findings)[7]

Globally, 2.9 million deaths are attributable to unsafe sex to date. The 4th largest cause of mortality in the world is HIV/AIDS, which can be acquired through unsafe sex. (2002 findings)[5]

Of the estimated 333 million new STD (sexually transmitted disease) cases that develop in the world every year, at least 1/3 occur in people under 25. (1997 findings)[4]

Health

Worldwide, about 500,000 deaths are attributable to unsafe injection practices in medical settings. (2002 findings)[5]

From the above statistics, one can objectively conclude the following:

In the United States, the number of medically uninsured individuals totals more than the combined populations of Texas, Illinois, and Michigan. About 1/4 of medium and large-sized corporations do not provide medical benefits for their employees. More than 1/4 of children under 3 do not receive all recommended vaccines. A significant number of children have unmet dental needs. One-third of prescription drug expenditures are not covered by any form of insurance. More than half of adults are overweight and more than 1/4 are obese. More than 7 million children are overweight. Every year, more than 1 million young people start smoking. Almost 10% of men abuse or are dependent upon alcohol. The number of people waiting for organ transplants totals more than the population of Newport Beach, California.

Worldwide, deaths attributable to alcohol total more than the entire population of Philadelphia, Pennsylvania. Deaths attributable to unsafe sex total more than the population of Chicago, Illinois. Tobacco causes almost 5 million deaths per year. Almost half of the men on the planet smoke. Every year, the number of individuals who become infected with STD's totals more than the entire population of the United States, and deaths that are attributable to unsafe injection practices equals the population of Las Vegas, Nevada.

Health

These statistics indicate that increasing numbers of individuals in the United States are now responsible for paying their own medical expenses – which is reflected in the statistics that 1/4 of medium and large-sized corporations do not provide medical benefits and 1/3 of prescription drug expenditures were paid out of pocket. The question then arises, are Americans sacrificing needed health care because of the cost? If many people are not getting the health care they truly need, will the number of those that are overweight continue to escalate along with the number of individuals who smoke and/or abuse (or are dependent upon) alcohol?

We're all familiar with the idea of the "American Dream." The idea that in this country opportunities are available that can allow a person of minimal means to become successful and happy.

But what if you get sick along the way. I mean, really sick. And you're nowhere near successful. You don't have health insurance. And you don't have the financial means to get medical care, so your health slowly deteriorates. Does that mean that your "American Dream" is over? You still yearn to be successful and happy, but you lack the vitality to help you achieve it.

It appears that the health care system in the United States is divided. One division is made up of medical practitioners and hospitals. Another division contains the pharmaceutical companies and other medical supply providers. The third division includes the insurance companies. The fourth division consists of employers who provide medical benefits. And the fifth, and largest, division is the general public whose health needs to be maintained. Each division wants to put its own needs first.

Health

We've all been raised to believe that a patient's needs come first. But the first four divisions consist of businesses. Businesses that want to make money. Can the various divisions of the health care system in the United States collaborate to create a structure in which each division's needs are met to a respectable degree while still maintaining the idea that a patient's needs come first? In addition, can they provide within that structure the accessibility of health care for every individual no matter what their income level?

I think most of us are compassionate people. If we knew someone who had health concerns, we would not ignore them or cast them aside. A new century citizen supports health care for everyone.

[1] U.S. Department of Health and Human Services, *Healthy People 2010*

[2] Bureau of Labor Statistics

[3] National Center for Health Statistics

[4] World Health Organization

[5] World Health Organization, *World Health Report 2002*

[6] National Institute on Alcohol Abuse and Alcoholism

[7] Organ Procurement and Transplantation Network

Is THE ENVIRONMENT our Highest Priority?

The Statistics

The largest form of air pollution is the presence of unacceptable levels of ground-level ozone, (an Air Quality Index of 100 or greater), which is created by motor vehicle exhaust and industrial emissions. In the United States, 120 million people live in areas with unacceptable levels. (2000 findings)[1]

In the United States, greenhouse gas emissions in 2001 were 11.9% higher than in 1990. These gases include carbon dioxide (released when solid waste, fossil fuels and wood products are burned), methane

New Century Citizen

(emitted during production of coal, natural gas and oil), nitrous oxide (emitted during agricultural and industrial activities), as well as hydrofluorocarbons, perfluorocarbons, and sulfur hexafluorocarbons (generated by industrial processes).[2]

Carbon dioxide emissions in the United States are projected to increase 1.5% per year from 2001 to 2025. Methane emissions are projected to increase 1% per year.[3]

Toxic air pollutants that originate from man–made sources (vehicles, factories, refineries, power plants) and are known or suspected to cause cancer or other serious health effects, such as reproductive effects or birth defects, include benzene, methyline chloride, perchlorethlyene, dioxin, asbestos, cadmium, mercury, chromium, and lead

The Environment

compounds, to name a few. Currently there are 188 toxic air pollutants that are released into the environment in the United States. (2003 findings)[4]

On March 13, 2001, President Bush declared that his administration would not seek to regulate power plants' emissions of carbon dioxide, citing an Energy Information Administration study that claimed that regulating these emissions could result in higher energy prices.[5]

SUV's (sport utility vehicles), minivans, and small trucks are less fuel efficient than small cars because these larger vehicles have lower gas mileage than cars and carbon dioxide emissions are directly related to the amount of fuel burned. In the United States, sales of these less efficient vehicles have increased sharply in recent years. (2003 findings)[5]

Nearly half of the world continues to cook with solid fuels (wood, coal, dung, agricultural residues), which are a large source of indoor air pollution. Indoor smoke from solid fuels can cause lung cancer, tuberculosis, cataracts, and asthma. (2002 findings)[6]

The U.S. National Water Quality Inventory for 2000 states that in 39% of assessed river and stream miles, in 46% of assessed lake acres, in 51% of assessed estuarine square miles, and in 78% of assessed Great Lakes shoreline miles, one or more designated uses such as fishing and/or recreation are impaired. Siltation, nutrients, bacteria, metals (primarily mercury), and oxygen-depleting substances are among the top causes of impairment. Pollution that is transported by precipitation and

The Environment

runoff from urban and agricultural land is the leading source of impairment.[4]

The U.S. National Listing of Fish and Wildlife Advisories listed 2,838 advisories for fish consumption or shellfish harvesting in effect in 2000. Mercury, PCB's, chlordane, dioxins, and DDT were responsible for 99% of all fish consumption advisories. Ten (10) of 28 coastal states reported prohibited, restricted, or conditionally approved shellfish harvesting in 1,630 square miles of estuarine waters.[4]

Drinking water contaminants in the United States include microbes (E coli, cryptosporidium, giardia, lamblia), radionuclides (radon, alpha emitters, beta/photon emitters, combined radium 226/228), inorganic contaminants (asbestos, barium, chromium, copper, mercury, nitrate, lead), synthetic organic contaminants (pesticides, herbicides), volatile organic contaminants, disinfectants, disinfection byproducts, and MTBE, a fuel additive. As of 2001, there are 91 contaminants regulated under the Safe Drinking Water Act.[4]

Approximately 1.7 million deaths worldwide are attributable to unsafe water, sanitation, and hygiene. Nine out of 10 such deaths are in children and virtually all of the deaths are in developing countries. (2002 findings)[6]

There are 1,220 sites on the U.S. National Priorities List, (a list of sites which release known or threatening hazardous substances, pollutants, or contaminants), that contain uncontrolled waste. States with the most sites include New Jersey with

The Environment

112, California with 96, Pennsylvania with 94, and New York with 90. (2003 findings)[4]

In the United States, over 20,000 hazardous waste generators produce over 40 million tons of hazardous waste each year. Varieties of hazardous waste include mixed waste (combination of radioactive and hazardous waste), liquid waste (including industrial and agricultural wastes), mining wastes, spent nuclear fuel, uranium mill tailings, used oil, solid waste, and household hazardous waste (including paints, cleaners, car batteries, and pesticides). (2003 findings)[4]

Approximately 220 million tons of municipal solid waste or garbage is generated in the United States each year. This means each person generates an average of 4.46 pounds of solid waste per day. (1998 findings)[4]

Currently there are 904 endangered species on the planet. (2003 findings)[7]

From the above statistics, one can objectively conclude the following:

Forty two (42)% of the U.S. population lives in an area with unacceptable levels of ground-level ozone. That's more than 1/3 of Americans. With current projections, carbon dioxide emissions will increase by 50% by the year 2033. Transportation and manufacturing practices produce byproducts that create toxic air pollutants. These pollutants can cause death and severe disease in humans. The executive branch of the U.S. legislature did not require power plants to regulate their emissions of

The Environment

carbon dioxide. An increasing number of automobile consumers in the United States do not consider fuel efficiency as an important factor in purchasing a vehicle. More than half of estuaries and Great Lakes shoreline as well as more than 1/3 of rivers, streams, and lakes that were assessed for water quality received a designation of impairment due to pollution. Per week, there were more than 54 advisories from the Fish and Wildlife Dept. Shellfish harvesting was reported prohibited, restricted, or conditionally approved in more than 1/3 of the coastal states. In the United States, there is an uncontrolled waste site for every 2,899 square miles. That is smaller than the area of Los Angeles County. There are an average of 400 hazardous waste generators per state. The United States generates 1,627 pounds of solid waste per year for every man, woman and child. Hazardous waste can be found almost anywhere, from one's personal residence to nuclear power plants, to mining operations to industrial and agricultural sites.

Nearly 50% of the world is exposed to indoor air pollution created by smoke from the burning of solid fuels. The number of deaths that are attributable to unsafe water, sanitation, and hygiene is greater than the population of Phoenix, Arizona. A significant number of animals and plants are in danger of becoming permanently extinct.

As years pass we are creating more pollution – considering the projections of carbon dioxide emissions, sales increases of vehicles that are less fuel-efficient, and the lack of power plant regulations for carbon dioxide emissions. Water quality is also compromised and hazardous waste is

The Environment

plentiful. With increased levels of pollution, will numbers of individuals with severe disease increase as well? Will increased levels of smog as well as fish and wildlife impairment also affect our quality of life (enjoyment of food and outdoor activities)?

Before Homo sapiens inhabited the earth, the only entities that existed were the atmosphere, the oceans and rivers, the land, the vegetation, and eventually the animals. When we see pictures of the earth from space, we can get an idea of how this new, unspoiled planet may have looked. Now, millions of years later, human beings have created toxins that contaminate that very same land, water and air. As our collective knowledge expanded, we became an industrial society. Many of these toxins are created as byproducts of the energy sources we need for important things like heat, electricity, and transportation. But somewhere along the way our increasing demand for production of these energy sources became more important than how it was affecting the planet - the planet that provides us sustenance through its vegetation, which is nourished by the now polluted land, water, and air.

    I have read that Native Americans believe that since a human's lifespan is infinitesimal compared to the lifespan of the earth, we human's hold the well-being of our environment in trust for future generations. In addition to our attempts to regulate the 188 toxic air pollutants, the 91 drinking water contaminants, and 40 million tons of hazardous waste, would it not be beneficial to create goals, and maybe even target dates, to begin eliminating some of these contaminants? This suggestion might create the need for some lifestyle changes. It might increase the price we pay for our energy. But as the 21st century progresses, do we

The Environment

want to be regulating more and more contaminants or striving to eliminate them instead? A new century citizen will be conscious of how he/she will leave the earth for future generations.

[1]National Center for Health Statistics, *Health, United States 2002*
[2]Energy Information Administration
[3]Energy Information Administration, *Annual Energy Outlook 2003 with Projections to 2025*
[4]Environmental Protection Agency
[5]Energy Information Administration, *United States Country Analysis Brief, October 2003*
[6]World Health Organization, *The World Health Report 2002*
[7]U.S. Fish and Wildlife Service

Is PERSONAL SAFETY our Highest Priority?

The Statistics

In 2000, 6.3 million violent crimes were committed in the United States including 261,000 rapes and 732,000 robberies.[1]

There were 19.3 million property crimes in the United States in that same year.[1]

In 2001, there were 15,980 murders committed in the United States, 63% with firearms. One-half of the offenders were under age 25.[1]

There are over 2.5 million applications processed every year in the United States for the purchase of a handgun. (1997 findings)[1]

In the United States, there were 2.6 million injured violent crime victims per year between 1992 and 1998.[1]

Sixty-seven (67)% of all victims of reported sexual assault in the United States were under 18 years of age for the years 1991 – 1996. Thirty-four (34)% of victims were under age 12.[1]

In 1997, a total of 2,100 juveniles were murdered in the United States, compared to 1,600 murdered in the mid-1980s.[2]

Personal Safety

Between 1980 and 1997, 75% of all juvenile murder victims in the United States between ages 12 and 17 were killed with a firearm.[2]

In 1999, teens in the United States between 12 and 18 years of age were victims of 186,000 serious violent crimes in school. Away from school there were 476,000 teen victims.[1]

In 2001, U.S. law enforcement agencies made an estimated 2.3 million arrests of persons under 18 years of age.[2]

Between 1992 and 2001, there was a 121% increase in juvenile arrests for drug abuse in the United States.[2]

New Century Citizen

In 1995, 1996 and 1999, 30 to 32% of U.S. students in grades 9-12 reported that someone had offered, sold, or given them an illegal drug at school.[3]

Between 1990 and 2001, 50% of all arsons in the United States were committed by juveniles.[2]

On any given day, U.S. juvenile courts handled nearly 4,500 delinquency cases in 2000 compared to 1,100 in 1960.[2]

Between 1984 and 1999, defendants charged with a drug offense in U.S. federal courts increased from 11,854 to 29,306. Sixty five (65)% of those charged in 1999 had previously been arrested and 50% had previously been convicted.[1]

Personal Safety

In 2002, 6.7 million people in the United States were on probation, in jail or prison, or on parole.[1]

On any given day in 1994, approximately 234,000 offenders convicted of rape or sexual assault were under care, custody, or control of U.S. corrections agencies. Nearly 60% of these sex offenders were under conditional supervision in the community.[1]

Of the 272,111 persons released from a U.S. prison in 15 states in 1994, an estimated 183,675 were re-arrested for a felony or serious misdemeanor within 3 years.[1]

From the above statistics one can objectively conclude the following:

    In the United States, the total number of annual violent crimes equals more than the population of Denmark. The sum of property crimes was double that amount. Two-thirds (2/3) of all murders were committed with firearms and 50% of murderers were age 25 or younger. Every year, the equivalent of two times the population of Dallas, Texas, applies to purchase a handgun. That same amount totaled the number of violent crime victims who were injured. Two-thirds (2/3) of sexual assault victims who reported the crime were under 18 years of age; 1/3 were under 12. About 1/3 more juveniles are being murdered now than were killed 15 years ago. Firearms were used in 3/4 of all juvenile murders whose victims were between 12 and 17 years of age. More than half a million teens were victims of serious violent crimes. Arrests of persons under 18 years old totaled more than the population of Nevada. The number of juveniles arrested for drug abuse has more than

Personal Safety

doubled in the course of 9 years. One-third (1/3) of all high school students reported that they had been offered, sold, or given an illegal drug at school. Half of all arsonists are juveniles. Juvenile delinquency cases have quadrupled over the last 40 years. Federal court drug offense cases have more than doubled during the last 15 years. Two-thirds (2/3) of those charged had been previously arrested and half (1/2) had previous convictions. The total number of convicted offenders under the jurisdiction of corrections agencies would fill Yankee Stadium more than 92 times. Two-thirds (2/3) of released prisoners were re-arrested for a felony or serious misdemeanor within 3 years in at least 15 states. About 1/4 of a million rapists or sexual assault offenders are under the care of corrections agencies on any given day.

More and more young people are committing crimes; this is reflected by the arrests of 2.3 million juveniles in the year 2001, as well as the fact that half of all murders are committed by individuals under 25 years old, half of arsons are committed by juveniles, juvenile arrests for drug abuse have doubled in less than a decade, and juvenile delinquency cases have quadrupled in the last 40 years. May one correlate the increase in juvenile drug abuse arrests with increases in juveniles committing murder and arson? With a significant number of handgun applications being processed every year, are more and more firearms going to get into the hands of young people? With 2/3 of prisoners getting re-arrested and half of drug offenders having prior convictions, will multiple offenses be the forecast for juvenile offenders? With approximately 6.3 million violent crimes taking place every year in the United States and 35% of the victims being injured, the personal safety of the average citizen is at risk.

Do you remember the feeling of being invincible when you were a teenager? The feeling like "nothing bad will ever happen to me." In the study of human development, it's actually considered a developmental stage that most of us go through at this age. Twenty to thirty years ago teens would go through this stage, but with the imposition felt from various authority figures (parents and teachers) most teens would not take too many risks due to the possibility of severe punishment. Somewhere along the way these authority figures lost their recognition from teens because young people today are taking more and more risks with little fear of punishment.

Where are the authority figures and role models for today's children? With a significant number of single-parent households, as well as two-income families, children sense the need to take on authority themselves at a much younger age. We've virtually taken away a teacher's authority to discipline their students. Now the only disciplinary avenue a teacher can pursue is to send the student to the principal's office with a threat of detention. Not even verbal reprimands on the part of the teacher can be considered for fear of a lawsuit. Many teens don't even see policemen as authority figures.

With the lack of authority figures, teens are feeling more the authority figure themselves. They have access to all kinds of resources on the internet. They have access to drugs and alcohol. Is it no wonder that more and more teens are taking greater risks and getting arrested? I think we need to

Personal Safety

reinstate some authority figures and role models in our children's lives. And reinstate the reality that severe consequences will occur when disregarding authority. A new century citizen will be a role model for our youth.

[1] Bureau of Justice Statistics
[2] Office of Juvenile Justice and Delinquency Prevention, *Statistical Briefing Book*
[3] National Center for Education Statistics, *Indicators of School Crime & Safety, 2001*

Is PEACE our Highest Priority?

The Statistics

In the last decade, more than 2 million children worldwide have died as a direct result of armed conflict. More than 3 times that amount have been permanently disabled or seriously injured. An estimated 20 million have been forced to flee their homes. More than 1 million children are orphaned or separated from their families.[1]

The following conflicts and their resulting consequences are taking place around the world:
Afghanistan – Millions of Afghans, many of them children, are still living in

temporary camps as a result of the war in 2001.[1]

Algeria – Armed bandits based in Mali attack southern Algerian towns. The border with Morocco is closed.[2] As a result of Algeria's civil war, 150,000 people died.[3]

Angola – In February 2002, the death of rebel leader Jonas Savimbi brought peace after a quarter century of nearly continuous warfare; however, the consequences of the conflict continue, including widespread use of land mines.[2]

Argentina – The region of the country adjacent to the border with Brazil and Paraguay is unruly with arms and drug trafficking.[2]

Peace

Armenia – A conflict exists with Azerbaijan over the Nagorno-Karabakh region; this conflict includes sporadic violence and use of land mines. Armenia's border with Turkey is closed. Armenia occupies 1/6 of Azerbaijan.[2]

Azerbaijan – This country supports 800,000 refugees as a result of a conflict with Armenia.[2]

Benin – Several villages are in a dispute with Nigeria.[2]

Bosnia and
Herzegovina – In this country, 12,000 NATO troops remain to monitor a peace agreement.[2]

Brazil – The region of the country adjacent to the border with Argentina and

Paraguay is unruly with arms and drug trafficking.[2]

Burkina Faso – The border region has become a staging area for Liberia and Cote d'Ivoire rebels.[2]

Burma – The government consists of a military regime.[2]

Burundi – In this country, 200,000 have perished in ethnic violence between Hutu and Tutsi factions. Hundreds of thousands of Burundians are refugees in neighboring countries. The country is also in conflict with the Democratic Republic of the Congo, Rwanda, and Uganda over the Great Lakes region.[2]

Peace

Cameroon – Armed clashes over Lake Chad occur with Chad, Niger, and Nigeria.[2]

Central African
Republic – A military coup deposed the civilian government in March 2003. The country's internal violence overlaps into Chad. Ethnic skirmishes take place along the border with Sudan.[2]

Chad – Chadian Aozou rebels reside in southern Libya. Border incidents occur at the border with Nigeria.[2]

Colombia – Guerrilla insurgents have been trying to overthrow the government. Several thousand paramilitary fighters have challenged the insurgents for

	control of their territory and the drug trade.[2] In 2002, a total of 3,500 people were killed and 2,000 kidnapped by guerrilla forces.[3]
Democratic Republic of the Congo –	The country is in the grip of a civil war. Uganda and Rwanda support rebel movements that occupy the eastern portion of the country. Ethnic groups and political rebels fight in the Great Lakes region despite UN peacekeeping efforts.[2]
Cote d'Ivoire –	Several thousand French and West African troops remain in the country to implement peace accords between rebels and the government.[2]

Peace

Eritrea – A UN peacekeeping operation monitors the border with Ethiopia where a 2.5-year border war took place and ended in 2000.[2]

Gaza Strip – The area is currently occupied by Israel. Widespread violence continues between the Israeli military and the Palestinian Authority over governance of the area.[2]

Georgia – Russian military bases still exist in the country. The ethnic areas of Abkhazia and South Ossetia have separated from the country.[2] A total of 100,000 citizens live in refugee camps due to a war in Chechnya. The Pankisi-Gorge region is a base for Chechen rebels.[3]

Guinea – Fighting is occurring among rebel groups in Guinea, Liberia, and Sierra Leone. Unrest in Sierra Leone has spilled into Guinea, creating a humanitarian emergency.[2]

Guinea-Bissau – A 1998 bloody civil war created hundreds of thousands of displaced persons. A war in Senegal results in cross-border raids on Guinea-Bissau.[2]

India – Involved in an armed standoff with Pakistan over the status of Kashmir.[2]

Indonesia – Refugees from conflicts in East Timor are in Indonesian camps.[2]

Peace

Iran – Thousands of Afghan refugees still reside in Iran.[2]

Iraq – Coalition forces remain in Iraq after the March 2003 invasion. Violence continues.[2]

North Korea – In December 2002, the government expelled UN monitors and repudiated a 1994 agreement to shut down nuclear reactors. The country maintains an army of about 1 million while relying on international food aid to feed its people North Koreans illegally migrate to China.[2]

Lebanon – Kizballah, a radical Shi'a party, maintains weapons. Syria maintains 16,000 troops in

	Lebanon (deployed during Lebanon's 16-year civil war).[2]
Liberia –	Supports the rebel insurgency in Sierra Leone. Border instabilities occur with Sierra Leone, Cote d'Ivoire, and Guinea.[2]
Libya –	The government consists of a military dictatorship led by Muammar al-Qadhafi.[2]
Mali –	Armed bandits in Mali attack southern Algerian towns.[2]
Moldova –	Russian forces remain in the country.[2]
Namibia –	Angolan rebels and refugees reside in this country.[2]
Nepal –	One hundred thousand (100,000) Bhutanese refugees reside in Nepal.[2]

Peace

Nigeria – Violence exists in the Niger Delta region. Over 10,000 deaths have occurred between the year 2000 and 2003.[3]

Pakistan – Thousands of Afghan refugees reside in Pakistan. Pakistan conducted nuclear weapons testing in 1998 in response to India's testing.[2]

Paraguay – The region at the border adjacent to Argentina and Brazil harbors Islamist militants. Arms and drug trafficking occurs.[2]

Philippines – Muslim insurgencies occur in the southern portion of the country.[2]

Russia – Conflict occurs in Dagestan between Russian forces and

	Islamic militants largely from Chechnya.[3]
Rwanda –	Involved in the Democratic Republic of the Congo's civil war. Rwanda participates in the fighting in the Great Lakes region, transcending the border with Burundi, The Democratic Republic of the Congo, and Uganda despite UN peacekeeping efforts.[2]
Senegal –	A separatist war in the Casamance region results in refugees and cross-border raids.[2]
Sierra Leone –	A UN peacekeeping force is in place as a recent 11-year civil war is coming to a close. However, fighting continues.[2]

Peace

Somalia – The country has no established permanent government. Numerous warlords and factions are fighting for control of the capital, Mogadishu.[2]

Sri Lanka – An ethnic war continues to fester after a ceasefire was declared in December 2001 between the government and the Liberation Tigers of Tamil Eelam.[2]

Sudan – Since 1989, an internal war has led to more than 2 million deaths and over 4 million people displaced. Although a cease-fire agreement is in place, the fighting continues. The current government consists of a military junta.[2]

Syria – The Golan Heights, previously a Syrian territory, is currently occupied by Israel.[2]

Turkey – The country's border with Armenia is closed because of the Nagorno-Karabakh dispute.[2]

Uganda – Sudanese rebel forces extend into Uganda. The country participates in the fighting in the Great Lakes region, transcending borders with Burundi, the Democratic Republic of the Congo, and Rwanda.[2]

United States – Effects of the September 11, 2001, terrorist attacks which resulted in 3,000 deaths at the World Trade Center, the Pentagon, and in Shanksville, Pennsylvania, are still

Peace

	being felt by the families and friends of the victims.[2]
Venezuela –	Drug-related conflicts occur along the Colombian border.[2]
Vietnam –	Armed encroachments take place along borders with Laos and Cambodia.[2]
West Bank –	Currently occupied by Israel. Widespread violence continues between the Israeli military and the Palestinian Authority over governance of the area.[2]
Zimbabwe –	Security forces are in place to repress opponents of the current prime minister.[2]

From the above statistics, one can objectively conclude the following:

More than 29 million of the world's children are personally experiencing the devastation of war. Fifty-four (54) of the world's 268 nations are experiencing armed conflicts and/or their consequences either within or transcending their borders.

With 1/5 of the world experiencing the havoc and strife of armed conflict, will the number of affected children increase at a significantly faster pace?

Disputes over which group is in power, who owns a particular piece of land, or which religious or ethnic group is superior, can easily turn into war. A war that can last for years. A war that can result in millions of deaths.

In 1992, a bloody war in Bosnia began between Bosnian Muslims, Catholic Croats, and Orthodox Serbs. Serbs carried out ethnic cleansing.

Peace

Murder, rape, and torture occurred. Muslim men were herded into concentration camps. A peace agreement was finally signed in 1995. Now, Catholics and Muslims live in the same cities. However, even though they've put down their weapons, a high level of animosity remains. This illustrates that peace can be negotiated, but ethnic and religious differences can still create impenetrable barriers.

Compared to the rest of the world, the United States is a fairly young country. As we've grown over the last 300 years or so, immigrants from all over the globe have flocked to our shores. We became a "melting pot." Because of this, we, as a country, have learned through difficult experiences of how important it is to accept those who have different cultural or religious beliefs than our own. We created a constitution that separates church and state to enforce this importance.

To the contrary, cultures in Africa, Asia, and Europe have existed for thousands of years. They are ensconced in the traditions and beliefs of their ancestors. Encouraging acceptance of another culture or religion to a country at war is a daunting task. Is it worth it? Do we want the numbers of children affected by armed conflict to continually increase? A new century citizen will encourage acceptance.

[1]UNICEF (2003 findings)
[2]CIA, *The World Factbook* (2003 findings)
[3]Energy Information Administration, *World Energy "Areas to Watch"* (2003 findings)

Is SERVICE our Highest Priority?

The Statistics

In the United States, 36.8 million people live in poverty. (2001 findings)[1]

The average poverty threshold for a family of four in the United States is an annual income of $18,104. (2001 findings)[2]

A total of 39% of children in the United States who live in single parent households headed by females live in poverty. (2001 findings)[2]

Just under 500,000 children live in households with child hunger in the United States. (2001 findings)[2]

An estimated 842,000 adults and children are homeless in the United States in any given week. That number may reach as high as 3.5 million over the course of a year. (2003 findings)[3]

A total of 556,000 children are in foster care in the United States. (2000 findings)[4]

There are 131,000 children in the United States waiting to be adopted. They have been in continuous foster care for an average of 44 months. (2000 findings)[4]

Worldwide, 73 million adolescents between 10 and 14 years of age are working. (1997 findings)[5]

Service

An estimated 174 million children under 5 years of age in the developing world are malnourished as indicated by low weight for age; 230 million are stunted. (1996 findings)[5]

Approximately 1/5 of the world's population live on less than U.S. $1.00 per day and nearly 1/2 live on less than U.S. $2.00 per day. (2002 findings)[6]

From the above statistics, one can objectively conclude the following:

In the United States, more than 1/3 of households headed by a single female parent live in poverty. Just under half of a million children experience hunger. Over the course of a year, the number of homeless adults and children can total more than the population of San Diego, California. More than half of a million children are in foster care, one fifth of whom have been waiting an average of almost four years to be adopted.

Worldwide, the number of adolescents between 10 and 14 who work totals more than the combined populations of France and Belgium. The number of children under 5 years of age who are malnourished or stunted totals more than the entire population of the United States. Nearly 3 billion people live on less than U.S. $2.00 per day. About 1.2 billion people live on less than U.S. $1.00 per day.

Nearly half of the world lives on less than U.S. $60 per month. With just $60 per month, what quality of food and shelter is available? Additionally, what quality of food and shelter is available for the 1.2 billion people who live on less than U.S. $30 per month?

Service

Many financial advisors suggest that one should budget 33% to 40% of one's income for housing expenses. For half of the world, that would be a maximum of U.S. $24 per month for rent. Any place you could rent for $24 per month more than likely would not include hot or cold running water, indoor bathroom facilities, heat, electricity, telephone service, or cable television. At least without those pesky amenities, bills for utilities or telephone won't need to be paid. The cost of gasoline would make owning a car prohibitive. That leaves $36 per month for food and any other necessities like medical care. Let's say that you decide to use $1 per day for food and try to save the remaining $6 for the future. This means that if you are lucky, you will have $72 saved in one year. Now your day-to-day life is about, "How can I get as much food as I can for $1?" This is your daily goal.

This doesn't sound like a description of the life of a human being. It sounds like the description of a scavenger - an individual who has a deficient quality of life. And half of the world lives in deficiency. How can we improve the lives of 3 billion people and elevate their reality from one of deficiency to at least an existence with some level of fulfillment - fulfillment being defined as access to shelter with heat, plumbing, and electricity as well as the provision of medical care and nourishing food?

Charities and service organizations have existed for many years that have helped the impoverished and fed the hungry. And there's no lack of trying on the part of these poverty-stricken individuals to try to dig themselves out of the hole.

Service

But it's difficult to dig when you don't have the right tools. There's an old saying that still rings true today. "Give a man a fish and he can eat for a day. Teach a man to fish and he can eat for a lifetime." If we added education to the definition of fulfillment, would individuals who now have a deficient life then be enabled to become independent and, therefore, self-reliant? The only question remains, where do we look for educators who will teach those experiencing deficiency? A new century citizen will encourage fulfillment and self-reliance through education for our fellow impoverished citizens.

[1]CIA, *The World Factbook*
[2]Federal Interagency Forum on Child and Family Statistics, *America's Children 2003*

[3] National Resource Center on Homelessness and Mental Illness

[4] Administration for Children and Families, *The AFCARS Report*

[5] World Health Organization

[6] World Health Organization, *The World Health Report, 2002*

Is MONEY our Highest Priority?

The Statistics

The following is a list of estimated retail and food service sales in the United States for 2001.[1]

Auto Dealers	$723 billion
Building Materials and Supplies	$251 billion
Clothing and Accessories Stores	$167 billion
Full Service Restaurants	$138 billion
Furniture and Home Furnishings	$91 billion
Radio, TV, and Other Electronics	$46 billion
Beer, Wine, and Liquor Stores	$30 billion
Sporting Goods Stores	$27 billion
Jewelry Stores	$24 billion
Computer and Software Stores	$24 billion

The average credit card debt in the United States is $8,400. (2003 findings)[2]

The top 2% of wealthiest individuals in the United States accounts for nearly 28% of total U.S. personal wealth. (1992 findings)[3]

The United States accounts for 5% of the world's population. It is the world's richest country, accounting for 21% of the gross world product. (2003 findings)[4]

Since 1972, U.S. high school seniors have been asked which values they felt were very important. In 1972, 26% of male seniors felt having lots of money was an important value. In 1982, 41.3% of males agreed and in 1992 the percentage rose to 45.3% of males. The corresponding view from

Money

females rose from 9.8% in 1972 to 24.1% in 1982 to 29.4% in 1992.[5]

From the above statistics, one can objectively conclude the following:

    Americans are spending billions of dollars and maintaining significant credit card debt. More than 1/4 of total personal wealth in the United States is held by only 2% of the wealthiest individuals. More than 1/5 of the gross world product is held by only 5% of the world's population. Over the past 30 years, more and more high school seniors feel that having lots of money is an important value.

    Americans are spending money whether they have it or not. Only a small percentage of the world's population possesses a significant amount of money. Will the totality of the world's wealth continue to be disproportionately divided?

I remember my first day of school back in the 1960s. I was terrified. My mother tried to ease my fear by telling me about all of the exciting things I was going to be learning like reading, writing, history, science, and math. She said that I'd also discover the worlds of art and music and maybe, someday, even learn a foreign language. She didn't mention that I was going to learn to value having lots of money. Then, again, I don't think they're teaching that in the 21st century, either. But almost half of male high school seniors and almost one-third of female high school seniors ascribe to that value. So they are learning it somewhere.

We tend to learn our values from our parents. We see what is important to mom and dad from a very young age and since a parent is a young person's greatest influence, we adopt their viewpoints. As we grow older, other influences come into play. Friends may begin to influence a young person. The media (e.g. television, music, film, the internet) may begin to influence a young person. So various forces impact an adolescent's value system. Forces over which a parent has no complete control. But is it beneficial for a parent to impose his/her values on their child? Isn't the learning process a teen goes through supposed to help them develop their own values, with a parent serving as a guide?

We like to ask preschoolers, "What do you want to be when you grow up?" And we'll hear responses like, "a fireman," "a policeman," "a teacher," etc. And as a teen enters high school the question then becomes, "What do you want to do with your life?" We encourage them to pinpoint an occupation as soon as possible so they can take the proper coursework. We've even created high schools that specialize in particular fields of study so students with that interest can get a jump-start on their career.

But I think we're missing something by asking these questions. I think a new query should be added. What if we asked our children, "***Who*** do you want to be when you grow up?" It might take some thought, but responses like "compassionate," "honest," "successful," or "hard-working," might be articulated. Then from a young age, children may learn to value who they want to be instead of what they want to have. Their focus will be shifted from external possessions to internal character. A new century citizen guides their children's value system by helping them focus on their internal character.

[1] U.S. Census Bureau
[2] Cardweb.com
[3] Internal Revenue Service, *Personal Wealth, 1992-1995*, by Barry W. Johnson
[4] CIA, *The World Factbook*
[5] National Center for Education Statistics, *Digest of Education Statistics, Tables and Figures*

Our Highest Priority

After 10,000 years of history as a society of human beings, our collective choices have created a global community where:

One-quarter of our fellowship can't read. And many of those who can most likely don't read at a proficient level. Parents are spending less time with their children, who are drinking alcohol, using illicit drugs, smoking cigarettes, and committing crimes in significant numbers. Many of us are mistreating ourselves. We're overweight, smoke cigarettes and abuse alcohol. And we're mistreating our planet as well by creating more pollution every year. The maltreatment continues with one-fifth of our global community experiencing armed conflict and half of our planet's citizens living in poverty.

These choices clearly indicate that education, relationships, health, the environment, personal safety, peace, and service are not our highest priority.

That leaves the category of money. In the United States, we're clearly spending it. Our young people value it. There is a disparity between those who have money and those who don't. Those who don't have it, want it. And those who do have it, want more.

Money takes precedence over education; we've created a world where higher education costs a lot of money.

Money takes precedence over our relationships; we've created a world where we spend more time at work than with our children or spouses.

    Money takes precedence over health; we've created a world where many of us pay high medical expenses out of pocket.

    Money takes precedence over the environment; we've created a world where keeping energy costs down is more important than limiting air pollution.

    Money takes precedence over personal safety; we've created a world where millions want to steal others' possessions.

    Money takes precedence over peace; we've created a world where millions want to steal others' power.

    Money takes precedence over service; we've created a world where there's a large disparity between those who have money and those who don't.

Clearly money is our highest priority. After reviewing these statistics, I wonder how I am contributing to these collective choices. I don't know anyone who lives on U.S. $2.00 a day. I don't create laws that pertain to education, health, or the environment. I'm not illiterate and I don't smoke or abuse alcohol. Perhaps I don't spend as much time with my family as I'd like, but I have to make a living. Perhaps I am concerned about my personal safety. Perhaps I do buy bottled water because I'm concerned about water pollution. Perhaps I do know people whose teens smoke cigarettes and drink alcohol. Perhaps I do know parents who have children in the military participating in an armed conflict.

Our Highest Priority

The truth is that I'm a very fortunate person. These statistics reflect the circumstances of many of my fellow global citizens. So the collective choices we've made as human beings do have an impact in some way on each of us. Would I personally choose money to be my highest priority? No, I would not. However, my actions do not reflect that. I would have to make some changes to re-prioritize my life. I would have to share my voice with those who have an impact on global concerns in the area of education, health care, peace, service, and the environment.

Money is our highest priority. Should we maintain this priority into the 21st century? Should this be the highest priority for a new century citizen? The canvas for the next 100 years still remains bare. What will be your resolution as a citizen of the new century?

About the Author

Mary Wallstrom, M.Ed., is an enthusiastic, creative educator with demonstrated talent in motivating people. She was born and raised in northeast Ohio. Degrees awarded her include a bachelor of arts from Ohio State University and a master's in education from the University of San Diego.

She is a seminar leader, a personal coach, and has taught at the university level. Her background includes designing workshops for under-privileged youth, serving as a career counselor, developing assessment tools, and producing a career-planning video. She has volunteered for the Make-A-Wish Foundation and the American Cancer Society.

    Ms. Wallstrom currently lives on the west coast. Her goal is to be a catalyst in aiding decision-makers at all levels as we enter the 21st century.

References

Chapter One – Education
National Center for Education Statistics
1990 K Street, NW
Washington, DC 20006
(202) 502-7300
http://nces.ed.gov

UNESCO Institute for Statistics
C.P. 6128
Succursale Centre-ville
Montreal, Quebec, H3C 3J7
Canada
(514) 343-6880
http://www.uis.unesco.org

Central Intelligence Agency
Office of Public Affairs
Washington, DC 20505
(703) 482-0623
http://www.odci.gov/index.html

Chapter Two – Relationships
U.S. Census Bureau
4700 Silver Hill Road
Washington, DC 20233-0001
http://www.census.gov

Office of Juvenile Justice and Delinquency Prevention
810 Seventh Street, NW
Washington, DC 20531
(202) 307-5911
http://ojjdp.ncjrs.org/index.html

References

Bureau of Labor Statistics
2 Massachusetts Avenue, N.E., Room 2860
Washington, DC 20212
(202) 691-5200
http://www.bls.gov

Federal Interagency Forum on Child and Family Statistics
 for copies of *America's Children 2002* write:
 Health Resources and Services Administration
 2070 Chain Bridge Road, Suite 450
 Vienna, VA 22182
http://www.childstats.gov

U.S. Department of Justice
950 Pennsylvania Avenue, NW
Washington, DC 20530-0001
http://www.usdoj.gov

Institute for Social Research
University of Michigan
Monitoring the Future Study
P.O. Box 1248
426 Thompson Street
Ann Arbor, MI 48106-1248
(734) 764-8354
http://www.monitoringthefuture.org

National Institute on Alcohol Abuse and Alcoholism
6000 Executive Blvd. – Willco Building
Bethesda, MD 20892-7003
(301) 443-3885 (office of the director)
http://www.niaaa.nih.gov/index.htm

References

The U.S. Department of Health and Human Services
200 Independence Avenue, S.W.
Washington, DC 20201
(202) 619-0257   (877) 696-6775
http://www.os.dhhs.gov

Chapter Three - Health
National Center for Health Statistics
3311 Toledo Road
Hyattsville, MD 20782
(301) 458-4636
http://www.cdc.gov/nchs/default.htm

World Health Organization
Avenue Appia 20
1211 Geneva 27
Switzerland
(+ 41 22) 791 21 11
http://www.who.int/en/

Organ Procurement and Transplantation Network
700 North 4th Street
Richmond, VA 23219
(804) 782-4876 (Data Request)
http://www.optn.org

References

Chapter Four – The Environment

Energy Information Administration, EI 30
1000 Independence Avenue, S.W.
Washington, DC 20585
(202) 586-8800
http://www.eia.doe.gov

Environmental Protection Agency
Ariel Rios Building
1200 Pennsylvania Avenue, N.W.
Washington, DC 20460
(202) 272-0167
http://www.epa.gov

U.S. Fish and Wildlife Service
4401 N. Fairfax Drive
Arlington, VA 22203-1610
(703) 358-1743
http://www.fws.gov

Chapter Five – Personal Safety

Bureau of Justice Statistics
810 Seventh Street, N.W.
Washington, DC 20531
(202) 307-0765
http://www.ojp.usdoj.gov/bjs/

References

Chapter Six – Peace
UNICEF House
3 United Nations Plaza
New York, NY 10017
(212) 326-7000
http://www.unicef.org

Chapter Seven – Service
National Resource Center on Homelessness and Mental Illness
Policy Research Associates, Inc.
345 Delaware Avenue
Delmar, NY 12054
(800) 444-7415
http://www.rrchmi.samhsa.gov

Chapter Eight – Money

CardWeb.com, Inc.
10 North Jefferson St., Suite 301
Frederick, MD 21701
(301) 631-9100
http://www.cardweb.com

Internal Revenue Service
Washington, DC
(202) 622-3300
http://www.irs.gov/index.html

Although the author and publisher have made every effort to ensure the accuracy and completeness of information contained in this book, we assume no responsibility for errors, inaccuracies, omissions or any inconsistency herein. All slights of people, places, or organizations are unintentional.